THE UNOFFICIAL
LORD OF THE RINGS
COOKBOOK

THE UNOFFICIAL
LORD OF THE RINGS
COOKBOOK

By
Tom Grimm

Photos by
Tom Grimm & Dimitrie Harder

REEL
INK
PRESS

For Ulrich "Uli" Peste,
who is Sam to my Frodo

Contents

Welcome to Middle-earth! 8

BREAKFAST
Millet Gruel 12
Beorn's Honey Cakes 14
Beren's Bread Flower 16
Breakfast Patties 18
Pancakes 20

SECOND BREAKFAST
Hobbiton Pumpkin Rolls 24
Cram 26
Fruitcake 28
Rivendell Fig Treats 30
Spud Cakes 32
Sam's Second Breakfast 34

ELEVENSES
Lembas 38
Farmer Maggot's Mushroom Ragout 40
Elvish Bread 42
Beorn's Baked Cheese 44
Home-Canned Peaches 46
Crickhollow Apple Cakelets 48
Túrin Turambar's Tarragon Chicken 51
Pumpkin Pastries 54
Bannock Bread 56

LUNCHEON
Oven Spuds in Chive Sauce 60
Smoked Beans Skillet 62
Ranger-style Quail 64
Brandywine Fish Casserole 66
Pippin's Lunch Snack 68
Garlicky Mussels from the Grey Havens 70
The Prancing Pony's Tater Soup 72
Bilbo's Famous Seed Cake 74
Fish in Bread Dough 76
Fluffy Mashed Potatoes 78
Pork Meat Pies 80

AFTERNOON TEA

Bilbo's Crunchy Cookies 84
Sweet Mini Bundt Cakes 86
Filled Oven Pears 88
Gandalf's Nut Pudding 90
Bilbo's Eleventy-First Birthday Cake 92
Sweet Chestnut Soup 96
The One Ring 98

DINNER

Haradrim Tagine 102
Root Vegetable Stew 104
Herbed Trout on a Stick 106
Sam's Coney Stew 108
Hobbit Shanks 110
Gimli's Salted Pork 112
Rosemary Lamb Skewers 114
Númenórean Gilthead Sea Bream 116
Juniper Roast Lamb 118
Orcish Hobbit Roast with Maggot Holes 120

SUPPER

Orcish Stick Bread 124
Tater Salad 126
Mirkwood Batwings 128
Dwarf-style Beetroot 130
Hobbit Head Cheese 132

DRINKS

Beorn's Honey Milk 136
Ent Potion 138
Miruvor 140
Athelas Tea 142
The Old Took's Hot Chocolate 144
Miruvóre 146
Orc Brew 148
Old Winyard's Mulled Wine 150

Acknowledgments 152
About the Author and Photographer 155
Recipe Index 156

Welcome to Middle-earth!

Stephen King, one of the most successful writers of all time, once said that writers are born to be writers—that an author's skills and trades can be learned up to a certain degree, but only "born" writers would sit at their typewriters even if writing was forbidden under penalty of death, just because they feel the urge to put down on paper all those stories that swirl around in their heads.

According to that definition, J. R. R. Tolkien was not a "real writer," since even at the peak of his success, he still considered writing drudgery and pursued it more as a hobby alongside his faculty work. So there was an obvious reason why it took him a full fifteen years to finish his magnum opus, *The Lord of the Rings*.

Tolkien's life was determined by his passion for language, not just in his career as a professor of Anglo-Saxon but also with regard to his creative work. Early on in his youth, Tolkien began to develop languages of his own, which later on became the bedrock of his entire artistry. His complete mythology actually arose from nothing but his intention to come up with a "real" background for his fictitious languages.

Tolkien's mythology first took shape in early 1917, when he came down with trench fever as a soldier in World War I and returned from the front lines in France back home to England. At that time, he started work on his "book of lost tales," an anthology of stories that would, many years later, become *The Silmarillion*, unfinished in his lifetime but later edited by his son Christopher Tolkien. In it, Tolkien put down the first roots of a new and unique world that he called, referring to Midgard from Norse mythology, Middle-earth.

In 1937, Tolkien presented Middle-earth for the first time to the public in *The Hobbit*, a book he originally wrote as a bedtime story for his children. The novel turned into a considerable best seller, so publisher Stanley Unwin asked Tolkien to come up with a sequel as soon as possible. Although Tolkien agreed, despite his dislike of the actual writing process, he had a much more mature book in mind from the very beginning—one that was supposed to appeal to grown-up readers as well. The title of this new Hobbit novel was *The Lord of the Rings*.

The rest is, as they say, history.

Tolkien considered his literary work primarily as an opportunity to research foreign peoples and cultures. It comes as no surprise that, despite all the fantastical aspects of his tales, the lives of Hobbits, Elves, Dwarves, and Men take center stage. Tolkien especially cared about the creature comforts of his heroes. His books are full of fond hints at food and drink, showing the author's enthusiasm for sumptuous feasts. After all, there is a good reason that both *The Hobbit* and *The Lord of the Rings* begin with elaborate banquets before the actual adventure starts. In Tolkien's eyes, food and drink stood for friendship, love, hope, and home.

This book offers an exceptional collection of a wide variety of foods and drinks derived from or inspired by Tolkien's works. So, if you were always dying to taste Bilbo's famous seed cakes, Sam's coney stew, the Prancing Pony's potato soup, or Túrin Turambar's tarragon chicken, here's your chance. Following the trails of Frodo, Aragorn, Gimli, Galadriel, Gollum, and all the other unforgettable characters from Tolkien's books, you'll be going on a culinary excursion through all of Middle-earth, from the peaceful Shire to the vast Elven forests and the caves of Mirkwood, all the way into the foothills of Mount Doom in the land of Mordor, where the shadows lie.

On that note, safe travels!

Tom Grimm

BREAKFAST

Millet Gruel 12

Beorn's Honey Cakes 14

Beren's Bread Flower 16

Breakfast Patties 18

Pancakes 20

Millet Gruel

Level	Prep Time	Cook Time
Easy	2 minutes	15 minutes

Serves 2

1 cup millet

1¼ cups water

1¼ cups milk

1 tablespoon cane sugar

2 tablespoons honey

1 teaspoon sea salt

2 tablespoons ground cinnamon

Fresh raspberries, for garnish

I. In a pot, bring the millet, water, and milk to a light boil, stirring constantly.

II. Add the cane sugar, honey, sea salt, and half of the ground cinnamon, mix well, and let simmer while stirring until the mixture takes on a nice mushy consistency, about 10 to 12 minutes.

III. Remove from heat and season to taste.

IV. Fill 2 breakfast bowls, top off with the remaining ground cinnamon, garnish with a couple of fresh raspberries, and serve.

Beorn's Honey Cakes

Level	Prep Time	Bake Time
Easy	15 minutes	20–25 minutes

Makes about 9

1 stick butter, softened, plus extra for greasing baking dish

1½ cups flour

1 teaspoon baking powder

½ cup blossom honey, plus extra for garnish

2 eggs

1 pinch salt

⅔ cup milk

Also needed:

Silicon honeycomb pull-apart cake mold or 9-cup nonstick muffin baking pan

I. Preheat oven to 325°. Grease baking dish with butter.

II. In a small bowl, combine the flour and baking powder.

III. In a mixing bowl, beat the softened butter with a hand mixer, and slowly drizzle in the honey. Add the eggs to the butter mixture one by one and incorporate thoroughly. Add the flour-baking powder mixture, salt, and milk and mix until batter is nice and smooth.

IV. Pour the batter into the prepared dish, smooth it, and bake for 20 to 25 minutes. Let the cakes cool in baking dish for a few minutes, then loosen them carefully from the mold and remove them.

V. Drizzle the cakes with honey before serving.

Tip
A wide variety of silicon honeycomb pull-apart cake molds can be found on the internet.

Beren's Bread Flower

Level	Prep Time	Bake Time
Medium	20 minutes, plus 70 minutes for rising	20–25 minutes

Makes 1 loaf

1 cup plus 1 tablespoon warm water

1 tablespoon fresh yeast

2 tablespoons sugar

1¾ cups flour

1 egg

2 teaspoons salt

1 tablespoon butter, softened, plus extra for greasing mold

1 egg yolk

Also needed:

Springform cake pan (about 9½ inches)

I. Pour 1 cup of warm water into a bowl. Crumble in the yeast, add the sugar, and stir to dissolve ingredients. Let sit for 10 minutes, until a fine layer of foam has formed on top.

II. Add the flour, egg, salt, and softened butter to a mixing bowl. Pour in yeast mixture and knead for at least 5 minutes into a smooth dough. Cover bowl with a clean dish towel, and let dough rest for about 50 minutes in a warm place until it has doubled in size.

III. Grease springform pan with butter.

IV. On a floured countertop, knead the dough one more time, then separate it into 7 pieces of equal size. Form each one into a ball and place them in the springform, arranging 6 along the edge and 1 in the middle with no gaps, so that the baked bread resembles a flower. Cover with dish towel and let rise for another 20 minutes.

V. Preheat oven to 350°.

VI. In a small bowl, combine the egg yolk with 1 tablespoon of water, use mixture to brush the dough balls in the springform pan. Bake until they are golden brown, approximately 20 to 25 minutes. Let cool for a few minutes, then loosen the bread from the pan.

Breakfast Patties

Level	Prep Time	Cook Time
Easy	15 minutes	10 minutes

Makes 6

1 pound potatoes

3 carrots

1 zucchini

1 onion, finely diced

1 egg

½ bunch of parsley, finely chopped

3 tablespoons bread crumbs

1 teaspoon fresh mint, finely chopped

Salt

Pepper

Vegetable oil

I. Peel the potatoes and carrots, wash them, and dry them off. Cut into rough pieces.

II. Wash the zucchini, take off the ends, and cut into rough pieces. Put them and the potatoes and carrots in the bowl of a food processor and grate them coarsely. (Alternately, grate them by hand.) Drain well in a colander.

III. Pour the grated vegetables into a bowl and add the onion, egg, parsley, bread crumbs, and mint. Season with salt and pepper, and mix well. Form into patties about 1 inch thick.

IV. In a nonstick skillet, heat 3 tablespoons of the vegetable oil on medium heat. Depending on the size of the skillet, add some of the patties and fry them to a golden brown color on each side (about 5 minutes). Place them on a plate covered with a sheet of paper towel to absorb excess grease.

V. Serve with cucumber raita (see page 114).

Pancakes

Level	Prep Time	Cook Time
Easy	10 minutes, plus 30 minutes for resting	15 minutes

Makes 8

5 tablespoons butter

1¼ cups milk

1¼ cups flour

2 eggs

1 pinch salt

1 teaspoon lemon zest

¼ cup sugar

Vegetable oil

Chocolate syrup, for garnish

Chocolate shavings, for garnish

Fresh raspberries, for garnish

I. Melt the butter in a pan on medium heat.

II. In a bowl, whisk together the milk and flour. Add the melted butter.

III. Beat the eggs in a separate bowl and add the salt, lemon zest, and sugar. Stir the egg mixture into the milk-flour mixture. Let the batter sit for 30 minutes.

IV. Heat some oil in a small nonstick pan. Add 2 to 3 tablespoons of the batter and swirl the pan so the batter thinly covers the entire bottom of the pan. Cook on medium heat. As soon as the upper side of the pancake begins to curdle and appear dry, turn it with a spatula and cook it until it is done. Drain the pancake on a paper towel. Cover with foil to keep warm. Repeat with the remaining batter.

V. Just before serving, generously drizzle the pancakes with chocolate syrup and garnish with chocolate shavings and fresh raspberries.

Tip

It is important to use just a small amount of butter and cook the pancakes on gentle heat for them to come out nice and fluffy.

SECOND BREAKFAST

Hobbiton Pumpkin Rolls 24

Cram 26

Fruitcake 28

Rivendell Fig Treats 30

Spud Cakes 32

Sam's Second Breakfast 34

Hobbiton Pumpkin Rolls

Level	Prep Time	Bake Time
Easy	90 minutes, including 1 ¼ hours for rising	20 minutes, plus 30 minutes for cooling

Makes 8

1¾ cups flour, plus extra

1 package dry yeast

1 teaspoon salt

1 tablespoon sugar

10 ounces pumpkin puree

½ cup warm water

1 egg

2 tablespoons water

Also needed:

Kitchen string

I. Line a baking sheet with parchment paper.

II. In a bowl, combine the flour, dry yeast, salt, and sugar. Add pumpkin puree and warm water and knead into a smooth dough. Cover bowl with a clean dish towel and set in a warm place to allow the dough to rise for 1 hour.

III. In the meantime, cut kitchen string into 8 pieces of about 20 inches each.

IV. Dust countertop with flour, then cut the risen dough into 8 pieces of equal size. Roll each piece into a ball. If the dough is too sticky, dust with some more flour.

V. Roll kitchen string in flour, then place each piece of string right under the center of one of the dough balls. Pull string up to the top of the roll and cross both ends. Turn the roll around and repeat process on the other side until the string separates the dough ball into 8 segments of about equal size. Tie the ends of the kitchen string loosely to allow the dough to rise some more.

VI. Place the rolls onto the prepared baking sheet, cover, and let rise for another 15 minutes.

VII. In the meantime, preheat oven to 350°.

VIII. In a small bowl, mix the egg with 2 tablespoons of water and brush the rolls with the mixture. Bake for about 20 minutes. Let cool for 30 minutes. Carefully remove kitchen string.

Cram

Level	Prep Time	Bake Time
Easy	15 minutes	15–20 minutes

Makes about 20

*10 ounces low-fat
cottage cheese*

½ cup whole milk

½ cup sugar

½ cup sunflower oil

1 egg

*2 cups cereal mix
(unsweetened)*

2 cups spelt flour

1 tablespoon baking powder

½ cup almond slivers

½ cup hazelnuts, sliced

I. Preheat oven to 350°. Line a baking sheet with parchment paper.

II. In a bowl, mix the cottage cheese, milk, sugar, oil, and egg until smooth.

III. In a separate bowl, combine the cereal, spelt flour, and baking powder. Add the almond slivers and hazelnuts slices, mix well, and add to the cottage cheese–milk mixture. Knead thoroughly.

IV. Using two tablespoons, arrange roughly rounded portions of dough on the prepared baking sheet.

V. Depending on their size, bake the cram for about 15 to 20 minutes until golden brown. Let cool on sheet for a few minutes. Store in an airtight container.

Fruitcake

Attention!
Uses Alcohol

Level	Prep Time	Bake Time
Easy	20 minutes, plus 12 hours for soaking	85–95 minutes, including time for cooling

Makes 1 loaf

1½ pounds apples, peeled, cored, and sliced

3 cups dried fruit, (such as figs, raisins, dates, apricots), roughly chopped

1¼ cups cane sugar

1¼ cups nuts, roasted and finely chopped

2 tablespoons gingerbread seasoning

1 pinch salt

½ tablespoon cocoa powder

¼ cup rum

Butter

1 cup flour, plus extra for dusting baking dish

1 tablespoon baking powder

Also needed:

Loaf pan
(about 12 by 4 inches)

I. In a large bowl, thoroughly mix the apples, dried fruit, sugar, nuts, gingerbread seasoning, salt, and cocoa powder. Add rum, combine well, cover tightly with plastic wrap, and let soak overnight.

II. Preheat oven to 350°.

III. Grease loaf pan with butter, then dust it with flour.

IV. In a bowl, combine 1 cup of the flour with the baking powder and add to the dried fruit–rum mixture. Stir into a smooth batter. Fill loaf pan, smooth surface of the batter, and bake for 70 to 80 minutes. Let cool in pan for 25 minutes, then overturn onto a cutting board.

Tip

The fruitcake tastes best when you tightly wrap it with plastic wrap immediately after cooling and let it sit at room temperature for a day.

Rivendell Fig Treats

Level	Prep Time
Easy	5 minutes

Makes 4

4 ripened figs

4 ounces cream cheese

1 teaspoon lemon juice

4 walnuts

Honey

4 small leaves fresh mint, for garnish

I. Wash the figs and pat them dry with a paper towel. Using a small knife, cut them into quarters without separating them at the bottom. Carefully press the lower half so the fruit opens like a blossom.

II. In a small bowl, mix the cream cheese and lemon juice until smooth.

III. Drop 1 to 2 tablespoons of the cream cheese mixture into the center of each fig, garnish with a walnut, and drizzle with honey. Top each treat off with a small mint leaf and serve immediately.

Spud Cakes

Level	Prep Time	Cook Time
Easy	25 minutes	15 minutes

Serves 4

For the spud cakes:

2 pounds potatoes
(waxy), washed, dried,
and roughly grated

1 onion, peeled and grated

2 eggs

1 pinch salt

3 tablespoons flour

1 pinch black pepper

10 tablespoons vegetable oil

*For the tomato-cream
cheese dip:*

6 ounces cream cheese

2 tablespoons milk

¼ cup dried tomatoes, roughly
chopped

1 garlic clove, roughly minced

Salt

Pepper

Fresh dill, finely chopped

Preparing the spud cakes:

I. In a large bowl, thoroughly mix grated potatoes and onion, eggs, salt, flour, and pepper with your hands.

II. Heat the oil in a frying pan on medium heat until it sizzles. Using a ladle, carefully add the potato mix (about 1 ladle per cake) and fry until the spud cakes have set (about 3 to 4 minutes). Turn and fry them on the other side for another 3 to 4 minutes, until golden brown. Place them on a plate covered with a paper towel to drain.

III. Serve with the tomato-cream cheese dip (see below).

Preparing the tomato-cream cheese dip:

IV. Blend the cream cheese, milk, dried tomatoes, and garlic in a food processor. In a small bowl, season the mixture to taste with salt, pepper, and freshly chopped dill. Keep it cool in refrigerator. Stir well before serving.

Sam's Second Breakfast

Level	Prep Time	Cook Time
Easy	15 minutes	45 minutes

Serves 4

For the beans:

3 tablespoons olive oil

2 onions, finely diced

2 garlic cloves, finely chopped

1 tablespoon tomato paste

½ cup vegetable broth

10 ounces white beans (canned), drained

5 ounces diced tomatoes (canned)

1 pinch cane sugar

1 squeeze lemon juice

Salt

Cayenne pepper

2 tablespoons parsley, freshly chopped

For the other delicacies:

Vegetable oil

8 green chile peppers

8 pointed peppers, small

8 tomatoes, small

8 sausages, small

8 bacon strips

4 minute steaks

2 cups forest mushrooms

Sea salt

Pepper, freshly ground

Herb butter (see page 53)

Preparing the beans:

I. In a sauté pan, heat the oil on medium heat. Add the onions and garlic and cook until translucent. Stir in the tomato paste and deglaze with the vegetable broth. Let reduce for 1 to 2 minutes. Add the beans and diced tomatoes and mix well. Let simmer for 10 minutes, stirring occasionally.

II. Season to taste with the cane sugar, lemon juice, salt, and cayenne pepper, and gently fold in the chopped parsley immediately before serving. Arrange on large plates alongside the other delicacies of this sumptuous second breakfast (see below) and serve immediately.

Preparing the other delicacies:

III. Preheat oven to 325°.

IV. In a nonstick pan, heat some oil on medium heat. As soon as it starts sizzling, add the chile peppers, pointed peppers, and small tomatoes. Roast them on all sides for 5 minutes, turning them over occasionally. Place them on a plate covered with a paper towel to drain, loosely cover with foil, and keep warm in oven.

V. Add fresh oil to the pan and heat. Fry the sausages, bacon, and steaks one after the other and keep warm in oven.

VI. Add oil to the pan and brown mushrooms on all sides for 5 minutes. To serve, sprinkle the vegetables with coarse sea salt and the mushrooms with sea salt and black pepper. Generously brush the warm steaks with herb butter.

VII. Arrange the beans together with the other delicacies on large flat plates and serve immediately.

ELEVENSES

Lembas 38

Farmer Maggot's Mushroom Ragout 40

Elvish Bread 42

Beorn's Baked Cheese 44

Home-canned Peaches 46

Crickhollow Apple Cakelets 48

Túrin Turambar's Tarragon Chicken 51

Pumpkin Pastries 54

Bannock Bread 56

Lembas

Level	Prep Time	Bake Time
Easy	15 minutes	15 minutes, plus 30 minutes for cooling

Makes 4

1½ cups flour

1 teaspoon baking powder

¼ teaspoon salt

1 stick butter

⅓ cup sugar

1 teaspoon vanilla sugar

1 teaspoon ground cinnamon

¼ cup heavy cream

4 small banana leaves

Also needed:

Kitchen twine

I. Preheat oven to 425°. Line a baking sheet with parchment paper.

II. In a large bowl, combine the flour, baking powder, and salt. Cut the butter into pieces and add to the flour mixture, mixing well. Then add the sugar, vanilla sugar, and ground cinnamon, mixing one more time. Add the heavy cream to the dough and knead well.

III. On a flour-dusted work surface, roll out the dough as thick as a finger and cut into four 3 by 4½ inch squares. Place them on the prepared baking sheet. Using a sharp knife, cut an *X* into each one to obtain the *Lord of the Rings* look. Bake for 12 to 15 minutes until light brown. Let cool for 30 minutes.

IV. Wrap each of the cooled lembas breads in one of the banana leaves and tie with twine. This not only looks great but also keeps the breads from drying out and getting hard.

Tip Stored in an airtight container, lembas keep almost indefinitely, but at least for a few weeks.

Farmer Maggot's Mushroom Ragout

Attention!
Uses Alcohol

Level	Prep Time	Cook Time
Easy	40 minutes, including time for soaking	30 minutes

Serves 6

For the bread dumplings:

9 day-old bread buns, cut into small cubes

1½ cups milk

1 tablespoon butter

2 large onions, finely diced

3 tablespoons fresh parsley, finely chopped

7 eggs

Salt

For the mushroom ragout:

Olive oil

1 onion, finely diced

4 ounces ham, cubed

7 cups forest mushrooms, diced

1½ cups forest mushroom stock

⅓ cup white wine

¼ cup heavy cream

1¼ cups crème fraiche

Salt

Pepper

2 tablespoons fresh parsley, finely chopped

Preparing the bread dumplings:

I. Place the bread cubes in a bowl. In a small pot, warm the milk on medium heat and pour on top of the bread cubes.

II. In a pan, melt the butter on medium heat. Add onions and parsley and cook for 2 to 3 minutes, then add them to the bread cubes. Add the eggs and salt and mix well. Let soak for 20 minutes at room temperature.

III. Using lightly moistened hands, form the dumplings and let steep in simmering, well-salted water for about 20 minutes. As soon as the dumplings are done, scoop them out of the water and let excess water drip off. Either serve fresh with the mushroom ragout (see below) or later, such as the next day when the dumplings are dry and firm. Slice them into pieces as thick as a finger and fry on both sides in butter.

Preparing the mushroom ragout:

IV. Heat some oil in a large pot. Add the onions and cubed ham, and brown on all sides (2 to 3 minutes). Add the mushrooms and cook uncovered until the liquid from the mushrooms has evaporated (approximately 10 minutes). Add the forest mushroom stock and reduce heat to low. Add the white wine and crème fraiche. Combine well and let reduce to desired consistency. Immediately before serving, season to taste with salt and pepper and fold in freshly chopped parsley.

Elvish Bread

Level	Prep Time	Bake Time
Medium	130 minutes, including time for rising	35–40 minutes

Makes 1 loaf

½ tablespoon fresh yeast

1 cup warm water

½ teaspoon sugar

1½ teaspoon salt

2¾ cups all-purpose flour, plus extra

I. In a medium bowl, crumble the yeast into the warm water. Add the sugar and stir until all ingredients have dissolved. Set aside for 10 minutes.

II. Add the salt and flour and knead into a smooth dough for at least 15 minutes. Cover with a clean dish towel, let dough rest for 10 minutes, then knead well for another 3 minutes. Cover again and let dough rise in a warm place for about 1 hour until the dough has almost doubled in size.

III. On a work surface lightly dusted with flour, flatten the dough a bit. Dust it with more flour. Pull one edge up and press it onto the middle of the flattened dough. Turn the dough and repeat from all sides. Repeat 2 to 3 times to give the dough as much tension as possible to help it keep its shape.

IV. Turn the dough upside down and, using your hands, mold it into desired shape. The surface of the bread should be smooth, with the folded side on the bottom. Let it rest for 30 minutes on a baking sheet lined with parchment paper.

V. Preheat oven to 475°. Place a heat-resistant bowl of water in oven.

VI. Using a sharp knife, cut a leaf pattern into the top of the dough. To do so, make an incision about ½ inch deep along the length of the loaf for the "stem," then add the "leaves" by making regular smaller crosscuts.

VII. Bake for 15 minutes. Reduce heat to 400° and bake for another 20 to 25 minutes until the loaf is golden brown.

Beorn's Baked Cheese

Attention!
Uses Alcohol

Level	Prep Time	Cook Time
Easy	10 minutes	About 30 minutes, depending on the type of cheese

Serves 1 to 2

One 8-ounce Camembert cheese wheel

¼ cup almond slices

¼ cup dried tomatoes

1 garlic clove, finely minced

2 tablespoons white wine

Pepper, freshly ground

¼ red chile pepper, thinly sliced into rings, for garnish

1 fresh baguette (preferably whole grain)

I. Preheat oven to 350°. Unwrap Camembert and place in a small baking dish. Bake for 15 minutes.

II. In the meantime, roast the almond slices in a small sauté pan on medium heat. Pour them into a small bowl. Set aside.

III. Using a sharp knife, finely chop the dried tomatoes. In a small bowl, combine them with the garlic and white wine. Season with pepper.

IV. Let the baked cheese cool. With a sharp knife, cut an *X* into the top and fold it out like a blossom (see photo). Pour the tomato mixture on top of the melted cheese, and garnish with the roasted almond slices and chile rings.

V. Serve with the baguette.

Home-Canned Peaches

Attention!
Uses Alcohol

Level	Prep Time	Cook Time
Easy	45 minutes	20 minutes

Makes 4 pints

4 pounds fresh peaches

2 vanilla beans

1 pound sugar

4 cups water

Juice of 2 lemons

½ cup rum

Also needed:

Four 1-pint pickle jars

I. Wash, peel, halve, and pit the peaches. (Set the peelings aside.) Rinse 4 pickle jars with hot water. Layer the peaches into the jars.

II. Halve the vanilla beans lengthwise and place them with the sugar, water, and peach peelings in a small pot and warm on medium heat. Let simmer for 5 minutes, stirring occasionally. Add the lemon juice and keep simmering until the sugar has dissolved.

III. Pour the peach syrup through a sieve into a bowl (reserving the vanilla bean pieces) and let it cool.

IV. Halve the vanilla bean pieces crosswise and add one half to each pickle jar. Pour the rum into the peach syrup, mix well. Pour mixture on top of the peaches in the jars and tightly seal them.

V. Place a dish towel in the bottom of a large pot, arrange the jars on top of it, and add at least 2 inches of water. Bring to a boil, reduce heat, and preserve the peaches for about 20 minutes in simmering water. Remove pot from heat and let jars cool off slowly in the water.

VI. Stored in a cool, dark place, the peaches will keep for up to a year.

Tip

To peel peaches easily, cut slightly into their skins using a sharp knife, place them in boiling water for 1 to 2 minutes, then chill them in ice-cold water.

Crickhollow Apple Cakelets

Level	Prep Time	Bake Time
Medium	2 hours, including time for resting	25–30 minutes

Makes 6

For the pastry:

1 stick butter, ice-cold

8 ounces low-fat cottage cheese

2 cups wheat flour

1 tablespoon sugar

1 pinch salt

For the filling:

5 apples, tart (about 1½ pounds)

3 tablespoons butter, plus extra for greasing baking molds

4 tablespoons cane sugar

4 tablespoons lemon juice

7 tablespoons water

1½ tablespoons cornstarch

1 teaspoon vanilla extract

1 pinch ground cinnamon

1 teaspoon lemon zest

1 egg yolk

Also needed:

6 tart molds (about 4½ inches)

Round cookie cutter (about 5½ inches)

I. Using a kitchen grater, finely shred the ice-cold butter into a mixing bowl. Add the cottage cheese, flour, sugar, and salt. Knead the mixture into a smooth pastry. Cover with plastic wrap and let rest in refrigerator for 30 minutes.

II. On a flour-dusted work surface, roll out the pastry into a rectangle. Fold in one-third of the pastry from one side, then from the other. Turn the pastry 90 degrees, roll out again, and fold one more time as described above. Cover in plastic wrap and cool in refrigerator for 1 hour.

III. In the meantime, prepare the filling. Peel the apples, core them, and cut them into small cubes.

IV. Melt butter in a pot on medium heat and add the apple cubes. Sprinkle them with the cane sugar and caramelize them slightly. Add the lemon juice and 2 tablespoons of water, and cook apples for about 5 minute, until they are almost soft.

V. In a cup, mix 3 tablespoons of water with the cornstarch, and add to the hot apple mixture. Stir well, bring to a boil, and remove from heat. Stir in the vanilla extract, ground cinnamon, and lemon zest. Let cool for a few minutes.

VI. In the meantime, preheat oven to 400°. Grease the tart molds with butter.

VII. On a lightly dusted work surface, roll out the pastry to a thickness of ¼ inch. Using a round cookie cutter (about 1 inch wider than the tart molds), cut out pastry circles. (The rim of a large drinking glass works just as well.)

Continued on next page

VIII. Line each mold with one of the pastry circles and carefully press on both the bottom and the sides. Cut off excess dough, spoon in apple mixture, and smooth the tops.

IX. Knead together the rest of the pastry, roll out, and cut into strips (each about 5 inches long). Layer them lattice-like on top of the filling (see photo), carefully pressing the ends along the edges.

X. In a small bowl, mix the egg yolk with the remaining 2 tablespoons of water, and brush the pastry strips. Bake the cakelets for 25 to 30 minutes until golden brown.

Túrin Turambar's Tarragon Chicken

Level	Prep Time	Cook Time
Easy	40 minutes	170 minutes, including time for resting

Serves 4

For the tarragon chicken:

2 tablespoons butter, melted

1 teaspoon ground paprika

1 teaspoon dried thyme

1 teaspoon pepper

1 teaspoon salt

1 bunch fresh tarragon, finely chopped

Whole corn-fed chicken, (about 3 pounds)

For the potato wedges:

4 tablespoons vegetable oil

2 garlic cloves, minced

1½ teaspoons salt

1½ teaspoons pepper

1½ teaspoon ground paprika (sweet)

2 pounds potatoes (waxy), quartered

Preparing the tarragon chicken:

I. Preheat oven to 400°. Place a baking sheet with some water in it onto bottom rack of oven to catch fat-drippings.

II. In a small bowl, combine the softened butter, paprika, thyme, pepper, salt, and three-fourths of the tarragon.

III. Remove the chicken's neck and innards. Wash the chicken with cold water, pat it dry with a paper towel, and rub in the seasoning mixture inside and out.

IV. Loosely cover the chicken with foil and cook for 45 minutes in oven. Remove foil, brush the chicken with the drippings, replace foil, and cook for another 45 minutes until the temperature measures 180° at the thickest part of the breast. In the meantime, occasionally brush the chicken with drippings.

V. Remove the chicken from oven and place it on a cutting board. Let it rest for at least 10 minutes before carving. Sprinkle with rest of the tarragon, and serve with potato wedges and herb-buttered corn on the cob (see below).

Continued on page 53

For the herb-buttered corn on the cob:

2 garlic cloves, minced

1 bunch mixed herbs (such as parsley, basil, rosemary, thyme, oregano), finely chopped

1 stick butter, softened

Salt

Cayenne pepper

4 sweet corn cobs, precooked

Preparing the potato wedges:

VI. Preheat oven to 350°. Line a baking sheet with parchment paper.

VII. In a large bowl, combine the oil, garlic, salt, pepper, and paprika. Add the potato wedges and mix until the potatoes are covered on all sides with the seasoning.

VIII. Spread the potato wedges onto the prepared sheet and bake them for 40 to 50 minutes until golden brown, turning them occasionally.

Preparing the herb-buttered corn on the cob:

IX. In a bowl, mix the garlic, chopped herbs, and butter. Season to taste with salt and cayenne pepper. Let the mixture chill.

X. Preheat oven to 425°.

XI. Generously coat the corn on the cob with the herb butter, wrap each one in foil, and cook them in oven for 20 minutes. Before serving, carefully open the "packages" (cautiously—they are steaming hot), brush with the drippings from foil, and add more herb butter.

Pumpkin Pastries

Level	Prep Time	Bake Time
Medium	2½ hours, including time for rising	25–30 minutes, plus time for cooling

Makes 8

For the dough:

3 cups flour, plus extra for dusting work surface

2 sticks butter

¾ cup sour cream

For the filling:

1 small Hokkaido pumpkin, deseeded and roughly pureed

Pumpkin seed oil

1 pinch salt

¼ cup sour cream

1 pinch pepper

1 pinch nutmeg

1 egg

For brushing:

1 egg

1 tablespoon milk

Also needed:

Round cookie cutter (4 inches)

Preparing the dough:

I. In a bowl, knead the flour, butter, and sour cream into a smooth pastry. Wrap up tightly in plastic wrap and cool for 2 hours in refrigerator.

II. Preheat oven to 350°. Line a baking sheet with parchment paper.

III. On a lightly dusted work surface, thinly roll out the pastry and cut out 8 circles using the cookie cutter. Arrange the pastry circles on the baking sheet, leaving some space in between.

Preparing the filling:

IV. In a large pot, combine the pumpkin pulp with the oil and the salt and cook on medium heat, stirring occasionally until soft. Using a hand blender, puree mixture as finely as possible. Add the sour cream and season with the pepper and nutmeg. Add the egg and stir the mixture well. Remove from heat and let slightly cool.

V. Drop 1 tablespoon of the pumpkin filling on top of each one of the pastry circles arranged on the baking sheet, fold them over once, and press on the edges, using either a fork or your fingers. With a knife, cut 3 small vertical slits into each turnover so hot air can escape during the baking process.

VI. In a small bowl, mix the egg and milk for brushing. Coat the pastries with egg-milk mixture and bake them for about 20 minutes until golden brown, turning them over once after 10 minutes. Let them cool on the sheet for 5 to 10 minutes and serve while they are still warm.

Bannock Bread

Level	Prep Time	Bake Time
Easy	20 minutes	15 minutes

Makes about 12

3 cups flour

1 tablespoon baking powder

1 pinch salt

¼ cup sugar

1 stick butter,
cubed and kept cold

¾ cup yogurt

½ cup raisins

Also needed:

Round cookie cutter
(4 inches)

I. Preheat oven to 325°. Line a baking sheet with parchment paper.

II. In a bowl, combine the flour and baking powder. Add the salt and sugar and mix well.

III. Add the butter and yogurt and thoroughly knead using a hand mixer fitted with dough hooks. Add the raisins and knead dough using your hands.

IV. On a work surface lightly dusted with flour, roll out the dough to a thickness of about 1 inch. Using a cookie cutter (or the rim of a glass of equal size), cut out dough circles and place them on the prepared baking sheet. Knead together the rest of the dough and cut out more pieces.

V. Bake for about 15 minutes until golden brown.

LUNCHEON

Oven Spuds in Chive Sauce 60

Smoked Beans Skillet 62

Ranger-style Quail 64

Brandywine Fish Casserole 66

Pippin's Lunch Snack 68

Garlicky Mussels
from the Grey Havens 70

The Prancing Pony's Tater Soup........... 72

Bilbo's Famous Seed Cake 74

Fish in Bread Dough 76

Fluffy Mashed Potatoes....................... 78

Pork Meat Pies 80

Oven Spuds with Chive Sauce

Level	Prep Time	Cook Time
Easy	5 minutes	45–60 minutes

Serves 4

1 cup crème fraiche

1 tablespoon lemon juice

*2 tablespoons
fresh chives, finely chopped,
plus more for garnish*

Salt

Pepper

4 large potatoes (floury)

Butter

I. Preheat oven to 400°.

II. In a small bowl, combine the crème fraiche with lemon juice and 2 tablespoons of freshly chopped chives. Season to taste with salt and pepper.

III. Wash, peel, and dry off the potatoes. Poke them on all sides with a knife. Wrap each of them, with a small piece of butter, in foil and place them on a rack in the middle of oven. Place a baking pan under the potatoes to catch any dripping butter. Bake the potatoes for 45 to 60 minutes, until a knife can be easily inserted into them. Remove them from oven. Use caution, as they will be hot.

IV. Let the potatoes cool off for a few minutes. Unwrap them, cut a large *X* in their tops, and push the sides apart to open. Generously fill the opening with chive sauce and sprinkle with chopped chives. Serve immediately.

Smoked Beans Skillet

Level	Prep Time	Cook Time
Easy	15 minutes, plus 1 hour for marinating	35 minutes

Serves 4

1 pound beef (top round)

3 onions, finely diced

1 clove garlic, finely chopped

2 tablespoons soy sauce

1 tablespoon granulated beef bouillon

2 pounds green beans

Salt

2 tablespoons oil

1 red bell pepper, julienned

8 ounces mixed mushrooms, chopped

½ cup roasted, salted peanuts, finely chopped

Pepper

Also needed:

Resealable freezer bag

I. Cut the meat into strips.

II. In a small bowl, combine one-third of the diced onions with the garlic, soy sauce, and bouillon. Place the mixture and the meat strips into a freezer bag and mix well. Let marinate in refrigerator for 1 hour.

III. In the meantime, wash and clean the beans and cut them into bite-size pieces. Place them in a pot and cover the beans with water. Add 1 teaspoon salt and bring to a boil on medium heat. Cover and let the beans simmer for about 15 minutes, then pour them into a colander and let them drain.

IV. Remove marinated meat from refrigerator. Heat the oil in a large skillet on medium heat and sear the meat in batches until nicely browned all over, about 5 minutes per batch. Remove the meat from the pan and keep it warm.

V. Place the rest of the onions in the pan and cook them in the remaining oil until translucent. Add the bell pepper and mushrooms, combine well, and cook for 5 minutes. Add the beans, stir, and cook for another 10 minutes. Then fold in the chopped peanuts and the meat and season to taste with salt and pepper.

Ranger-style Quail

Level	Prep Time	Cook Time
Easy	10 minutes	30 minutes

Serves 4

1 pound baby potatoes

¼ red bell pepper, julienned

¼ yellow bell pepper, julienned

¼ green bell pepper, julienned

6 tablespoons olive oil

8 quail

Salt

Pepper, freshly ground

Ground paprika

1 organic lemon, cut into 8 wedges

8 stems thyme

8 garlic cloves, unpeeled and smashed

8 bay leaves

Coarse sea salt

Also needed:

Kitchen twine

I. Preheat oven to 425°. Line a baking sheet with parchment paper.

II. Thoroughly wash the potatoes, dry them with a paper towel, and place them into a bowl. Add the bell peppers and 4 tablespoons of oil and mix well. Spread potatoes and bell peppers on the prepared baking sheet, and bake them on middle rack of oven for 10 minutes.

III. In the meantime, season the quail inside and out with salt, pepper, and paprika. Fill each quail with 1 lemon wedge, 1 stem of thyme, 1 garlic clove, and 1 bay leaf. Tie the legs with kitchen twine.

IV. In a skillet, heat the remaining oil on high heat and brown the quail on all sides. Add them to the vegetables on the baking sheet and cook for another 20 minutes.

V. Sprinkle the potatoes with the sea salt before serving.

Brandywine Fish Casserole

Level	Prep Time	Cook Time
Easy	10 minutes	35 minutes

Serves 4 to 5

1½ pounds potatoes

Salt

4 fillets plaice (about 3 ounces each), cut into bite-size pieces

1 pound fillets pollack, cut into bite-size pieces

3 tablespoons lemon juice

½ pound zucchini, sliced

2 red onions, thinly sliced

Pepper

Butter for greasing the casserole

1 cup heavy cream

¼ cup crème fraiche

1 cup cheese (such as cheddar or Mexican-style blend), grated

Fresh chervil, finely chopped

Also needed:

Flat casserole pan (about 8 by 12 inches)

I. In a pot filled with heavily salted water, boil the potatoes for 15 minutes. Drain and cool them in cold water, then peel and slice them.

II. Place the fish in a large bowl and drizzle with the lemon juice. Add the zucchini, red onions, and potatoes, carefully combine, and season well with salt and pepper.

III. Preheat oven to 400°. Grease casserole with butter.

IV. In a separate bowl, whip the cream. Fold in the crème fraiche, and season with salt and pepper. Pour on top of the fish-potato mixture, carefully combine, and pour the mixture into the casserole. Smooth the surface, evenly sprinkle with the cheese, and cook in preheated oven for about 20 minutes.

V. Garnish with the chervil and serve.

Pippin's Lunch Snack

Level	Prep Time	Cook Time
Easy	10 minutes	53 minutes

Serves 4

2 pounds fresh kale

Salt

1 tablespoon clarified butter

2 shallots, finely diced

4 cups vegetable broth

1 tablespoon granulated bouillon

3 tablespoons Dijon mustard

1 pound potatoes, peeled and diced

2 smoked pork chops, cut into bite-size pieces

4 sausages (such as bratwurst or frankfurters)

3 tablespoons oats

Celery salt

Pepper, freshly ground

Nutmeg, freshly grated

I. Wash the kale very thoroughly.

II. In a large pot, bring heavily salted water and the kale to a boil and let simmer for 3 minutes. Pour the kale into a colander, rinse it with cold water, let it drain, then coarsely chop it and remove the hard stems.

III. Melt the clarified butter in a large pot on medium heat. Add the shallots and cook them until translucent. Add the chopped kale, vegetable broth, bouillon, and mustard and simmer on low heat for 25 minutes.

IV. Add the potatoes and pork to the pot and stir. Pierce sausage casings so they won't split open while cooking, then add them. Cover and simmer for another 25 minutes, stirring occasionally.

V. When the kale is done, add the oats. Season with the celery salt, pepper, nutmeg, and more mustard if needed.

Tip — Oats will thicken the dish. For a thinner consistency, omit them.

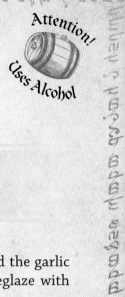

Garlicky Mussels from the Grey Havens

Level	Prep Time	Cook Time
Easy	15 minutes	30 minutes

Serves 4

1 tablespoon vegetable oil

4 garlic cloves, minced

2 shallots, finely diced

⅓ cup white wine

2 cups vegetable broth

2 cups water

14 ounces diced tomatoes (canned)

1 bunch of mirepoix, finely chopped

2 tablespoons sherry, medium dry

1 tablespoon granulated beef bouillon

1 teaspoon pepper

⅓ cup heavy cream

1 teaspoon celery salt

4 pounds mussels

½ red chile pepper, thinly sliced

Fresh parsley, coarsely chopped

I. Heat the oil in a large pot on medium heat. Add the garlic and shallots and cook them until translucent. Deglaze with the white wine, and let reduce for 2 to 3 minutes.

II. Add the vegetable broth, water, tomatoes, mirepoix, sherry, bouillon, pepper, cream, and celery salt and bring to a boil, stirring constantly.

III. Soak the mussels in a large bowl of water and scrub them, scraping off pocks and beards. (Discard any mussels that are not tightly closed.) Rinse them well after scrubbing.

IV. Add the mussels and sliced chile pepper to the pot and let simmer for 12 to 15 minutes. Immediately before serving, sprinkle in some chopped parsley and season the cooking liquid to taste. (Remove any mussels that did not open during cooking.)

The Prancing Pony's Tater Soup

Level	Prep Time	Cook Time
Easy	10 minutes	45 minutes

Serves 3 to 4

1 tablespoon clarified butter

2 shallots, finely chopped

3 garlic cloves, minced

1 pound fresh forest mushrooms, choppped

4–5 large potatoes, peeled and roughly cubed

1 bunch green onions (white parts only), finely sliced

2 bay leaves

5 dried allspice berries

2 cups vegetable broth

2 cups water

2 tablespoons butter

2 tablespoons flour

1 tablespoon dried marjoram

1 tablespoon granulated beef bouillon

Salt

Pepper

Fresh parsley, finely chopped

I. Melt the clarified butter in a large pot on medium heat. Add the shallots and garlic, and cook until translucent. Add the mushrooms and sauté for 5 minutes. Add the potatoes, green onions, bay leaves, and allspice berries to the pot, and combine well. Add the vegetable broth and water, and simmer for 20 to 25 minutes until the potatoes are done, stirring occasionally.

II. In the meantime, melt 2 tablespoons of butter in a pot on low heat. Dust the melted butter with 2 tablespoons of flour and cook for 2 to 3 minutes, constantly stirring, until the roux is creamy and smooth. If it is too dry, work in some of the cooking liquid little by little.

III. Stir the roux into the soup. Season with the marjoram, bouillon, salt, and pepper. Simmer for another 10 minutes. Remove the bay leaves and allspice berries before serving.

IV. Garnish with the chopped parsley.

Bilbo's Famous Seed Cake

Level	Prep Time	Bake Time
Easy	15 minutes	45–50 minutes

Makes 1

1½ sticks butter, softened, plus extra

2⅔ cups flour, sifted, plus extra

¾ cup sugar

3 eggs

1 teaspoon baking powder

1 pinch salt

1 tablespoon ground almonds

1 tablespoon milk

2 teaspoons caraway seeds

Also needed:

Loaf pan
(about 10 by 5 inches)

I. Preheat oven to 350°. Grease the loaf pan with butter, then dust it with flour.

II. Using a hand mixer in a bowl, beat the butter and sugar until light and fluffy. Incorporate the eggs one by one.

III. In a separate bowl, combine the flour with baking powder and stir into butter-sugar mixture. Add the salt, almonds, and milk, and mix well. Fold in the caraway seeds.

IV. Pour the batter into the loaf pan, and smooth the surface. Bake for 45 to 50 minutes. The cake is done when a toothpick inserted into the middle comes out clean. Let the cake cool in the pan before carefully loosening and removing it.

Fish in Bread Dough

Level	Prep Time	Bake Time
Easy	15 minutes	30 minutes

Serves 2

1 organic orange

1 trout (about 14 ounces)

Salt

Pepper

1 stick cinnamon

14 ounces pizza dough

1 egg yolk

1 tablespoon water

Caraway seeds (optional)

I. Preheat oven to 350°. Line a baking sheet with parchment paper.

II. Rinse the orange with hot water, dry it, and zest it using a kitchen grater. Then, cut the orange in half and the halves into wedges, each about ¾ of an inch wide.

III. Rinse the trout inside and out and dab it dry using a paper towel. Make a couple of incisions on one side, each about ¼ inch deep. Salt and pepper the outside and inside of the trout, then rub with the orange zest. Fill with the cinnamon stick and orange wedges.

IV. Unroll the pizza dough onto a lightly dusted work surface and place the trout lengthwise in the center. Fold the dough over the trout from the bottom and the top so the edges overlap in the middle. Carefully press the dough around the trout and seal both ends tightly.

V. In a small bowl, mix the egg yolk and water.

VI. Place the fish in dough on the prepared baking sheet, brush the dough with the egg mixture, sprinkle with the caraway seeds, if desired, and bake for about 30 minutes until golden brown.

Fluffy Mashed Potatoes

Level	Prep Time	Cook Time
Easy	5 minutes	40 minutes

Serves 4

2 pounds potatoes (floury)

Salt

¾ cup milk

¾ cup heavy cream

5 tablespoons butter, cut into pieces

Pepper, freshly ground

1 pinch nutmeg, freshly grated

I. Peel the potatoes and cut them into quarters.

II. In a large pot, bring heavily salted water to a boil on medium heat. Add the potatoes and let simmer for about 30 minutes, until a knife can easily be inserted into them.

III. Drain the potatoes, put them in a large bowl, and let them steam. Then use a potato masher to mash them until there are small chunks of potato.

IV. Add the milk, cream, and butter to the bowl and fold into the mixture until the mashed potatoes are still coarse but creamy and fluffy. Season with salt, pepper, and a hearty pinch of grated nutmeg.

Pork Meat Pies

Level	Prep Time	Cook Time
Easy	2½ hours, including time for chilling	60 minutes

**Makes 3 big
or 6 small pies**

For the pastry:

2¾ cups flour

2 sticks butter, cut into pieces,
plus extra for greasing
pie molds

Salt

2 eggs

2 tablespoons water

For the filling:

1½ pounds ground pork

6 ounces ham, cubed

2 tablespoons bread crumbs

3 shallots, finely diced

2 garlic cloves,
minced

1 egg

Salt

Pepper, freshly ground

1 pinch nutmeg

Egg yolk for brushing pastries

Also needed:

Three 20-ounce or
Six 10-ounce pie molds

Preparing the pastry:

I. Sift the flour into a bowl, forming a crater in the middle. Add the butter, salt, eggs, and water in the crater, knead the ingredients together, form the pastry into a ball, cover with plastic wrap, and cool for 2 hours in refrigerator. In the meantime, prepare the filling.

Preparing the filling:

II. Place the ground pork, cubed ham, bread crumbs, shallots, garlic, and egg in a bowl. Season with salt, pepper, and nutmeg.

Preparing the pies:

III. Preheat oven to 350°. Separate the pastry into either 3 or 6 parts of equal size, depending on the size of pie molds. Roll the pieces out to a thickness of about ¼ of an inch.

IV. Grease the pie molds with butter. Cut either 3 or 6 round pieces from the pastry that are a little larger than the molds and fill each mold with one piece. Spoon the filling into them almost to the top. Smooth the surface.

V. Roll out the remaining pastry and cut 3 or 6 circles a little larger than the molds. Cover the filling with the pastry circles and press on the protruding edges to seal the pies. Cut an *X* into the top of each.

VI. Lightly beat the egg yolk and brush the pies with it. Bake for about 60 minutes, until the pies are golden brown. Let them cool for a few minutes. Carefully remove the pies from the molds and enjoy either warm or cool.

AFTERNOON TEA

Bilbo's Crunchy Cookies............................84

Sweet Mini Bundt Cakes..........................86

Filled Oven Pears 88

Gandalf's Nut Pudding............................ 90

Bilbo's Eleventy-First
Birthday Cake...92

Sweet Chestnut Soup............................. 94

The One Ring 96

Bilbo's Crunchy Cookies

Level	Prep Time	Bake Time
Easy	15 minutes	10–12 minutes

Makes about 20

2 sticks butter, softened

¾ cup brown sugar

1 cup cane sugar

2 teaspoons vanilla sugar

2 eggs

1 cup flour

1 teaspoon baking powder

1 pinch salt

1 cup oats

1 cup chocolate chips

½ cup walnuts, roasted and finely chopped

I. Preheat oven to 350°. Line 2 baking sheets with parchment paper.

II. In a bowl, beat the butter, sugar, cane sugar, and vanilla sugar until light and fluffy. Incorporate the eggs one by one.

III. In a separate bowl, mix flour, baking powder, and salt. Slowly add the flour mixture to the butter-sugar mixture and combine carefully. Stir in the oats, chocolate chips, and chopped walnuts.

IV. Roll the pastry into 2-inch-long "sausages" about as thick as a child's finger. Arrange them onto the baking sheets, leaving space between them, as they will melt into oval shapes during baking.

V. Bake cookies for 10 to 12 minutes until golden brown. Move them onto a cooling rack.

Sweet Mini Bundt Cakes

Attention!
Uses Alcohol

Level	Prep Time	Bake Time
Easy	20 minutes	20 minutes

Makes 6

For the mini bundt cakes:

1 stick butter, softened, plus extra for greasing baking pan

½ cup sugar

1 pinch salt

2 eggs

1 cup flour

2 teaspoons baking powder

⅓ cup egg liqueur

For icing:

1 cup powdered sugar

3 tablespoons egg liqueur

Also needed:

6-cavity mini fluted tube baking pan

Preparing the the mini bundt cakes:

I. Preheat oven to 325°.

II. Grease the baking pan's molds with butter.

III. In a mixing bowl, using a hand mixer, beat the butter, sugar, and salt until light and fluffy. Incorporate the eggs one by one.

IV. In a small bowl, combine the flour and baking powder. Add it to the butter mixture and stir in the egg liqueur until the batter is smooth and creamy.

V. Pour the batter into the molds of the pan and smooth the tops. Bake for about 20 minutes; a toothpick inserted in the center of a mini cake should come out clean. Let cool in pan, then carefully remove the mini cakes.

Preparing the icing:

VI. To serve, whisk the powdered sugar and egg liqueur in a small bowl and pour the mixture over the mini cakes.

Filled Oven Pears

Level	Prep Time	Cook Time
Easy	5 minutes	20 minutes

Serves 4

2 fresh pears

1 cup mixed nuts

¼ cup dried fruit, roughly chopped

3 tablespoons raisins

4 tablespoons honey

2 tablespoons vanilla sugar

I. Preheat oven to 350°. Line a baking sheet with parchment paper.

II. Wash the pears and dry them off with a paper towel. Cut into halves and core them.

III. In a small bowl, mix the nuts, dried fruit, raisins, honey, and vanilla sugar.

IV. Arrange the pear halves on a baking sheet and generously add the nut-and-dried-fruit mixture into the hollows where the cores had been, loosely cover the pears with foil, and bake for about 20 minutes.

Gandalf's Nut Pudding

Level	Prep Time	Cook Time
Easy	5 minutes	10 minutes, plus 2 hours for cooling

Serves 4

4 cups milk, plus extra

⅓ cup hazelnuts, coarsely chopped

⅓ cup walnuts, coarsely chopped

⅔ cup coconut flakes

⅓ cup almonds, coarsely chopped

½ cup cane sugar

3 tablespoons ground cinnamon

⅔ cup cornstarch

Walnuts, for garnish

I. Add the milk, hazelnuts, walnuts, coconut flakes, almonds, cane sugar, and cinnamon to a pot. Combine and bring to a boil on medium heat, stirring constantly. Simmer until the coconut flakes and sugar have dissolved.

II. Mix the cornstarch with a small cup of milk and add to the pot. Reduce heat to low and continue to simmer, constantly stirring, until the mixture starts to thicken.

III. Divide the pudding into 4 dessert bowls and cool in refrigerator for 2 hours.

IV. Garnish with walnuts and serve.

Bilbo's Eleventy-First Birthday Cake

Level	Prep Time	Bake Time
Hard	2 hours, plus time for cooling	75 minutes

Makes 1 cake

For the large flan base (about 10 inches):

6 eggs

1¼ cups sugar

1 pinch salt

1⅓ cups flour

1 teaspoon baking powder

½ cup almonds, ground

For the small flan base (about 7 inches):

4 eggs

¾ cup sugar

2 teaspoons vanilla sugar

1 pinch salt

1¼ cups flour

1 teaspoon baking powder

Preparing the large flan base:

I. Preheat oven to 350°. Line the bottom of the large springform pan with parchment paper.

II. Using an electrical hand mixer on high, beat the eggs, sugar, and salt for at least 4 minutes.

III. In a separate bowl, combine the flour with the baking powder and almonds and fold it into the egg mixture. Pour the batter into the prepared springform pan, smooth the surface, and bake in lower third of oven for about 45 minutes. Loosen the flan base from the springform pan immediately and carefully turn over onto a cooling rack covered with parchment paper. Let cool.

Preparing the small flan base:

IV. Line the bottom of the small springform pan with parchment paper.

V. In a bowl, beat the eggs, sugar, vanilla sugar, and salt with an electrical hand mixer on highest setting for at least 3 minutes.

VI. In a separate bowl, combine the flour and baking powder and fold into the egg mixture. Pour the batter into the prepared springform pan, smooth the surface, and bake in lower third of the oven for about 30 minutes. Loosen the flan base from the pan immediately and carefully turn it onto a cooling rack covered with parchment paper. Let cool.

Continued on next page

For the buttercream:

1¼ cups Cream of Wheat

½ cup sugar

1 tablespoon vanilla sugar

4 cups milk

2 sticks butter,
room temperature

For the ganache:

1 cup heavy cream

20 ounces white chocolate,
coarsely chopped

For decoration:

¼ cup fresh raspberries,

¼ cup fresh blackberries

¼ cup blueberries

Fresh Physalis

2 white fondant sheets
(about 16 ounces), room
temperature

Also needed:

2 springform pans (about 10
and 7 inches, respectively)

2 cake rings (about 10 and 7
inches, respectively)

Edible flowers (such as roses,
baby's breath, violets)

Small birthday cake candles

Preparing the buttercream:

VII. Add the Cream of Wheat, sugar, vanilla sugar, and milk to a pot and bring to a boil, stirring constantly. Let simmer until the mixture thickens to a porridge-like consistency. Remove from heat and let cool.

VIII. Using a hand mixer, beat the butter until creamy, add to the mixture, and mix until creamy. Place the mixture in refrigerator.

Preparing the ganache:

IX. In a small pot, bring the cream to a boil and remove it from heat immediately. Add the chopped chocolate and whisk until it has dissolved.

Assembling the cake:

X. Horizontally split the cooled-off flan bases in half. Place the lower halves onto cake plates, with the cut surfaces facing up. Fit matching cake rings over them.

XI. Spread the buttercream onto both flan bases, smooth the buttercream, and place the upper halves on top. Place them in refrigerator for at least 1 hour to set the buttercream.

XII. In the meantime, wash the berries and carefully dab them dry with paper towels. Cut the flower stems down to just over 1 inch. Set a couple of rose leaves aside.

XIII. Remove the cakes from refrigerator and carefully slide a knife blade along the edges inside of the cake rings to loosen them. Coat the cakes evenly with ganache. Spread one of the fondant sheets over each cake, then press it on gently, smooth it carefully, and cut off all protruding pieces with a knife.

XIV. Place the smaller cake in the center on top of the larger one. Fill in the gap between both cakes with the flowers, which not only enhance its appearance but also help cover any unevenness. Decorate edge of the lower cake with berries, Physalis, and rose leaves.

XV. Arrange the candles on top of the cake, light them immediately before serving, and enjoy the admiration in everybody's eyes!

Sweet Chestnut Soup

Attention!
Uses Alcohol

Level	Prep Time	Cook Time
Easy	5 minutes	25 minutes

Serves 4 to 5

4 tablespoons butter

2 shallots, finely diced

1 garlic clove, minced

14 ounces chestnuts, precooked, peeled, and finely chopped

⅓ cup white wine

⅓ cup walnuts, finely chopped

3 cups vegetable stock

3 ounces fresh chanterelles

Salt

Pepper

1 cup heavy cream

1 teaspoon ground cinnamon

1 teaspoon sugar

I. Melt 3 tablespoons of butter in a pot on medium heat. Add the shallots and garlic and cook until translucent, about 3 minutes. Add the chestnuts and brown them on all sides for 3 to 4 minutes. Deglaze with the white wine and bring to a boil for just a moment. Add the walnuts and vegetable stock and cover and simmer for 10 minutes, stirring occasionally.

II. In a separate pan, melt 1 tablespoon of butter on high heat and brown the chantarelles on all sides for about 3 minutes. Season with salt and pepper and place on a plate lined with a paper towel to drain.

III. Pour the cream into the soup. Add 1 teaspoon each of the ground cinnamon and sugar and finely puree using a hand blender. Season to taste with salt and pepper.

IV. To serve, garnish soup with the browned chantarelles.

Tip

Substitute a dash of vinegar for the white wine if you prefer.

The One Ring

Level	Prep Time	Bake Time
Medium	30 minutes, plus 2 hours, 40 minutes for rising	15–20 minutes

Makes 2 loaves

1 cup walnuts

1 package dry yeast

1¼ cups warm water

5 cups dark flour (such as spelt)

1 teaspoon salt

2 teaspoons honey

I. Preheat oven to 325 degrees. Spread the walnuts onto a baking sheet lined with parchment paper and roast in oven for 6 to 10 minutes. Let them cool off, then roughly chop them.

II. In a small bowl, dissolve the yeast in warm water, and let it sit for 10 minutes to activate.

III. In a separate bowl, combine the flour and salt. Add the roasted walnuts, yeast mixture, and honey, and knead into a dough for a couple of minutes. Roll the dough into a ball, cover it with a clean dish towel, and let it rise for 2 hours.

IV. Place the dough on a work surface lightly dusted with flour and cut it into 2 pieces of equal size. Form them into oblong loaves, twisting the dough a few times by turning it piece by piece into opposite directions using both hands (see photo). Form each into a ring and place them on a baking sheet lined with parchment paper. Cover and let rise for another 40 minutes.

V. Preheat oven to 450°.

VI. Bake for 15 to 20 minutes until the crusts are nicely browned.

DINNER

Haradrim Tagine 102

Root Vegetable Stew 104

Herbed Trout on a Stick 106

Sam's Coney Stew 108

Hobbit Shanks 110

Gimli's Salted Pork 112

Rosemary Lamb Skewers 114

Númenórean Gilthead Sea Bream 116

Juniper Roast Lamb 118

Orcish Hobbit Roast with
Maggot Holes 120

Haradrim Tagine

Level	Prep Time	Cook Time
Easy	10 minutes	45 minutes

Serves 4

3 tablespoons olive oil

3 tablespoons tomato paste

½ teaspoon harissa (spice mixture)

1 teaspoon salt

1 teaspoon pepper

8 chicken drumsticks

1 red onion, finely diced

2 garlic cloves, minced

1 piece fresh ginger (about 1 inch), finely chopped

6 dried apricots, coarsely chopped

4 ounces chickpeas (canned), drained

4 ounces yellow lentils (canned), drained

4 tablespoons pomegranate seeds

3 tablespoons raisins

1 stick cinnamon

¾ cup vegetable stock

⅓ cup orange juice

Juice of ½ organic lemon

2 stems cilantro, finely chopped

2 stems mint, finely chopped

Also needed:

Tagine (optional) or deep frying pan

I. In a bowl, mix 1 tablespoon of oil and the tomato paste, harissa, salt, and pepper.

II. Rinse the chicken drumsticks with cold water, pat them dry with paper towels, and generously brush them with the tomato-harissa mixture on all sides.

III. Add 2 tablespoons of oil to a deep frying pan on medium heat. Cook the onions, garlic, and ginger for 2 to 3 minutes. Add the drumsticks and brown them on all sides. Add the chopped apricots, chickpeas, lentils, pomegranate seeds, raisins, and cinnamon stick, stirring well. Pour in the vegetable stock and orange juice, and bring to a boil, stirring constantly. Add the lemon juice, cover, and let simmer for 20 minutes. Uncover and simmer for another 20 minutes.

IV. Immediately before serving, add chopped cilantro and mint. Remove the cinnamon stick.

Tip

When using a tagine, proceed as directed, but leave the lid on the pot during the entire cooking time.

Root Vegetable Stew

Level	Prep Time	Cook Time
Easy	10 minutes	35–45 minutes

Serves 5 to 6

1 tablespoon vegetable oil

2 shallots, thinly sliced into rings

1 garlic clove, minced

1 tablespoon fresh ginger, finely chopped

2 pounds carrots of varied colors, sliced

10 ounces parsnips, sliced

6 ounces parsley root, sliced

10 brown mushrooms, thinly sliced

¼ stick celery, thinly sliced

6 cups vegetable stock

5 juniper berries

2 bay leaves

Celery salt

Pepper

½ teaspoon ground cinnamon

Caraway seeds

Smoked sausage (as much as desired)

½ red chile pepper, thinly sliced (optional)

Fresh parsley, finely chopped

2 tablespoons pomegranate seeds

I. Heat the oil in a large pot on medium heat. Add the shallots and garlic and cook until translucent. Add the ginger and cook it for a moment. Add the carrots, parsnips, parsley root, mushrooms, and celery, mix well, and cook for about 5 minutes, stirring occasionally.

II. Deglaze with the vegetable stock. Add the juniper berries and bay leaves. Season with the celery salt, pepper, cinnamon, and caraway seeds. Add the whole sausages and, optionally, the red chile pepper. Simmer uncovered for about 30 minutes, until the vegetables are done. Remove the bay leaves and juniper berries.

III. Stir in the chopped parsley and pomegranate seeds. Slice the sausage immediately before serving.

Herbed Trout on a Stick

Level	Prep Time	Cook Time
Easy	20 minutes	30–35 minutes

Makes 4

4 trout, kitchen-ready
(about 10 ounces)

Salt

Pepper, freshly ground

1 teaspoon vegetable oil, plus
extra for greasing sticks

1 shallot, finely chopped

3 garlic cloves, minced

2 tablespoons olive oil

Zest of 1 organic lemon

½ bunch of Italian parsley,
finely chopped

2 stems of rosemary,
finely chopped

1 stem of sage,
finely chopped

Also needed:

4 sharpened sticks from
nontoxic wood (such as
hazelnut, willow, beech)

Charcoal briquettes,
or embers from a campfire

I. Prepare fuel for fire.

II. Thoroughly wash the trout inside and out and pat them dry with paper towels. Season them with salt and pepper on the inside and outside.

III. In a frying pan, heat the vegetable oil on medium heat. Add the shallots and garlic and cook until translucent. Remove from heat and let cool slightly.

IV. In a small bowl, mix the olive oil, lemon zest, parsley, rosemary, and sage. Fill the fish with some of the herb mixture, and coat them with the remaining amount.

V. Grease the pointy ends of the sticks with vegetable oil. Carefully insert them into the trout mouths and skewer them by guiding the stick along the backbone until it comes out at the tail end.

VI. As soon as the fuel is ready, hold the fish, backs down, 1 to 1½ feet above heat for about 20 minutes. Then turn them so the belly sides face down and grill them for another 15 to 20 minutes. (Take care to keep the trout from charring.)

VII. Carefully remove skewers before serving.

Tip

The fish can also be cooked the traditional way in an oven. To do so, wrap each trout in foil adding olive oil and lemon slices, then cook them in an oven preheated to 400° for 15 to 20 minutes.

Sam's Coney Stew

Attention!
Uses Alcohol

Level	**Prep Time**	**Cook Time**
Easy	30 minutes	2 hours

Serves 4 to 5

2 pounds rabbit meat
1 stick cinnamon
2 stems rosemary
4 stems thyme
2 bay leaves
1 tablespoon vegetable oil
3 shallots, finely diced
3 garlic cloves, minced
2 large carrots, finely diced
1 cup celery root, finely diced
1 leek, thinly sliced
10 ounces potatoes,
    peeled and diced
10 ounces mixed forest
    mushrooms, diced
⅓ cup dry red wine
2 tablespoons cognac
1¾ cups vegetable stock
3 juniper berries
Salt
Pepper
1 teaspoon pimento
¼ cup chocolate (80% cocoa),
    roughly chopped
Kitchen twine

I. Thoroughly rinse the rabbit meat with cold water, remove any fat, and dice.

II. Using kitchen twine, tie the cinnamon stick, rosemary, thyme, and bay leaves into a small bouquet.

III. Add the oil to a large pot on medium heat. Cook the shallots and garlic until translucent. Add the rabbit meat and brown it on all sides for 5 to 6 minutes. Add the carrots, celery root, leek, and potatoes and cook for 5 minutes, stirring occasionally. Add the mushrooms and cook for 5 minutes. Deglaze with the red wine and cognac.

IV. Add the vegetable stock to the pot, then the juniper berries and the herb bouquet, reduce heat to low, and let simmer for at least 2 hours.

V. When the meat just melts on your tongue, remove the herb bouquet and juniper berries from the pot. Season the stew to taste with the salt, pepper, and pimento, then add the chocolate to the pot and stir until it has dissolved.

Hobbit Shanks

Attention! Uses Alcohol

Level	Prep Time	Cook Time
Easy	15 minutes	2 hours

Serves 4

4 small veal shanks

Salt

Pepper

1 tablespoon flour

2 tablespoons olive oil

1 onion, finely diced

2 sticks celery, finely diced

1½ cups celery root, peeled and cubed

6 ounces potatoes, peeled and quartered

1½ cups carrots, sliced

8 ounces brown lentils (canned), drained

3 cups vegetable stock

14 ounces diced tomatoes

¼ cup red port

Zest of 1 lemon

2 garlic gloves, very finely minced

¼ bunch Italian parsley, finely chopped

Also needed:

Roasting pan

I. Preheat oven to 400°.

II. Rinse the veal shanks with cold water and pat them dry with paper towels. Season with salt and pepper. Sift the flour onto the shanks.

III. In a roasting pan large enough to arrange the veal shanks side by side, heat 1 tablespoon of oil. Add the shanks and roast them on all sides until golden brown, 8 to 10 minutes. Remove them from the pan and place them on a paper towel to drain.

IV. Add the remaining oil to the roasting pan and heat it. Add the onions and cook them until they are translucent. Add the diced celery sticks, celery root, potatoes, carrots, and lentils, stir well, and cook briefly. Deglaze with the vegetable stock. Place the veal shanks back in the roasting pan, bring to a simmer, and cover.

V. Braise veal shanks in lower third of oven for about 75 minutes. Add the diced tomatoes and port. Season the liquid to taste with salt and pepper, and braise for another 20 to 30 minutes until the meat starts to fall off the bones.

VI. In a small bowl, mix the lemon zest, garlic, and parsley. Stir into the vegetables immediately before serving. Place one-fourth of the vegetables on each plate and arrange one of the veal shanks on top of each one.

Gimli's Salted Pork

Level	Prep Time	Cook Time
Easy	5 minutes	90 minutes

Serves 2 to 3

For the salted pork:

2 salted pork hocks
(about 1 pound)

1 bay leaf

5 black peppercorns

2 juniper berries

1 teaspoon vinegar

1 onion, quartered

For the sauerkraut:

2 tablespoons vegetable oil

1 onion, finely diced

14 ounces sauerkraut
(canned)

1 bay leaf

3 juniper berries

1 teaspoon granulated
beef bouillon

1 teaspoon caraway seeds

Salt

Pepper

Preparing the salted pork:

I. Rinse the pork hocks with cold water, place them in a large pot, and cover the meat with water. Add the bay leaf, peppercorns, juniper berries, vinegar, and the quartered onion, cover, and simmer for about 1 hour.

Preparing the sauerkraut:

II. After 30 minutes, heat the oil in a large pot on medium heat, add the diced onion, and cook until translucent. Add the sauerkraut, bay leaf, juniper berries, bouillon, and caraway seeds, and season to taste with salt and pepper. Add 1 ladle of the stock from the other pot to the sauerkraut, combine well, cover, and simmer, stirring occasionally, until the hocks are done.

III. After the hocks have cooked for 1 hour, remove them from the stock, and nest them in the sauerkraut. Cover and cook for another 30 minutes. If necessary, add some of the stock occasionally.

IV. Remove the bay leaf and juniper berries from the sauerkraut before serving.

Rosemary Lamb Skewers

Level	Prep Time	Cook Time
Easy	20 minutes, plus 13 hours for marinating and resting	10 minutes

Makes 4

For the lamb skewers:

2 pounds lamb meat
(from the hip)

3 stems thyme,
very finely chopped

2 stems oregano,
very finely chopped

1 stem rosemary,
very finely chopped

6 basil leaves,
very finely chopped

Zest of ½ organic lemon

2 garlic cloves,
very finely chopped

1 teaspoon salt

6 tablespoons olive oil

1 tablespoon vegetable oil

Pepper

Salt flakes (optional)

For the cucumber raita:

½ cucumber

1 tablespoon salt

1 cup Greek yogurt

2 teaspoons herb blossoms

1 pinch ground cumin

1 teaspoon lemon juice

Also needed:

Metal skewers

Preparing the lamb skewers:

I. Trim the lamb meat of sinew and fat, cut the meat into bite-size pieces, and place it in a large bowl.

II. In a small bowl, combine the thyme, oregano, rosemary, basil, lemon zest, garlic, salt, and olive oil. Pour this marinade on top of the meat and mix well. Cover it with plastic wrap and store it in refrigerator for 12 hours.

Preparing the cucumber raita:

III. In the meantime, finely grate the cucumber into a bowl and combine it with 1 tablespoon of salt. Let sit for 30 minutes, drain off excess water, place grated cucumber in a clean dish towel, and wring it out until the cucumber pulp is as dry as possible.

IV. Place the cucumber pulp in a bowl. Add the yogurt, herb blossoms, ground cumin, and lemon juice, and mix well. Cool in refrigerator.

Cooking the lamb skewers:

V. Remove the marinated meat from the refrigerator and let it sit at room temperature for 1 hour. Place the pieces of meat onto the metal skewers.

VI. Heat a large cast-iron pan on medium heat and add 1 tablespoon of vegetable oil. Tilt the pan to coat its entire bottom with oil. Brown the lamb skewers 3 to 4 minutes, depending on desired degree of doneness, on both sides.

VII. Season the lamb skewers with freshly ground black pepper and sprinkle a few salt flakes on top of them. Serve with the cucumber raita.

Númenorean Gilthead Sea Bream

Level	Prep Time	Cook Time
Easy	15 minutes	30 minutes

Serves 2

1 gilthead sea bream
(about 1 pound)

Salt

Pepper

2 to 3 stems sage

2 stems rosemary

2 to 3 stems basil

1 to 2 garlic cloves,
finely minced

3 tablespoons white wine

4 tablespoons olive oil

I. Preheat oven to 400°.

II. Wash the fish, pat it dry with a paper towel, and sprinkle it with salt and pepper inside and outside. Make a couple of incisions into the back of the fish, each about 1 inch deep.

III. Pick the sage, rosemary, and basil leaves off the stems. Fill the fish with half of the herbs and finely chop the rest and mix, in a small bowl, with the garlic, white wine, and oil, and season to taste with salt and pepper.

IV. Line an oven-safe cooking dish with a large piece of parchment paper. Place the fish on top of it, generously brush it with herb mixture, and wrap it into the parchment paper.

V. Cook in oven for 30 minutes. Transfer the package with the fish inside onto a platter, carefully open it, and serve hot.

Juniper Roast Lamb

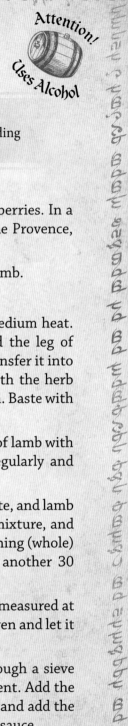

Attention!
Uses Alcohol

Level	Prep Time	Cook Time
Easy	20 minutes	90–100 minutes, including time for resting

Serves 4

15 juniper berries

1 teaspoon salt

1 teaspoon pepper

1 teaspoon herbs de Provence

4 garlic cloves, finely minced

1 leg of lamb (about 3 to 4 pounds)

5 tablespoons olive oil

2 tablespoons butter

3 shallots, finely chopped

1½ cups red wine

2 tablespoons cognac

2 tablespoons tomato paste

1½ cups lamb stock

½ cups heavy cream

Sauce thickener (optional)

Also needed:

Large casserole dish

I. Using a mortar, finely pestle half of the juniper berries. In a bowl, combine them with the salt, pepper, herbs de Provence, and garlic.

II. Roughly cut the sinew and fat off of the leg of lamb.

III. Preheat oven to 425°.

IV. Heat oil and butter in a large frying pan on medium heat. Add the shallots and cook until translucent. Add the leg of lamb, and sear it on all sides for 5 to 6 minutes. Transfer it into a large casserole, generously sprinkle the meat with the herb mixture, and cook for 25 minutes in preheated oven. Baste with the meat juices.

V. Reduce oven heat to 350°. Loosely cover the leg of lamb with foil and cook for another 45 minutes. Turn it regularly and baste it with the juices.

VI. In a bowl, mix the red wine, cognac, tomato paste, and lamb stock, generously brush the leg of lamb with the mixture, and pour the rest of it into the casserole. Add the remaining (whole) juniper berries to the sauce. Cover and cook for another 30 minutes, basting occasionally.

VII. As soon as the core temperature reaches 151° measured at the thickest part of the meat, remove it from the oven and let it rest for 10 minutes before cutting.

VIII. In the meantime, strain the meat juices through a sieve into a small pot and bring to a boil for just a moment. Add the heavy cream, season to taste with salt and pepper, and add the sauce thickener if needed. Serve the meat with the sauce.

Orcish Hobbit Roast
with Maggot Holes

Level	Prep Time	Cook Time
Easy	5 minutes	60 minutes

Serves 4

1 tablespoon butter, plus extra for greasing pan

2 onions, finely diced

1½ cups bread cubes

1 bunch Italian parsley, finely chopped

1 tablespoon marjoram, finely chopped

1 teaspoon salt

Pepper, freshly ground

2 pounds ground pork

1 egg

6 ounces bacon strips

Cooked white rice, for garnish

Also needed:

Loaf pan (about 8 by 7 inches)

I. Melt 1 tablespoon of butter in a pan on medium heat. Add the onions and cook until translucent, about 5 minutes. Add the bread cubes, parsley, and marjoram, season with salt and pepper, combine well, and cook briefly. Remove from heat and let cool for a few minutes.

II. Place the onion-bread mixture and the ground pork in a large bowl. Add the egg and thoroughly knead with your hands until all components are well combined.

III. Preheat oven to 350°.

IV. Grease loaf pan with butter. Cover bottom and sides of pan with the bacon strips. Gently press the meat mixture into the pan, leaving about 1 inch between the top of the mixture and the rim of the pan. Smooth the surface and fold the protruding bacon over the mixture.

V. Cook for about 45 minutes, until the meat is done all the way through. If you like, pour the pan juice into a small pot and use it as a gravy base.

VI. Carefully turn the loaf onto a cutting board and garnish with white rice for "maggot holes."

SUPPER

Orcish Stick Bread 124

Tater Salad 126

Mirkwood Batwings 128

Dwarf-style Beetroot............................... 130

Hobbit Head Cheese 132

Orcish Stick Bread

Attention!
Uses Alcohol

Level	Prep Time	Cook Time
Easy	20 minutes, plus 1¼ hours for rising	75 minutes

Makes 8

3¾ cups flour

1 package dry yeast

1 teaspoon salt

1 teaspoon garlic salt

1 teaspoon Italian herbs

1 pinch sugar

1 cup warm water

3 tablespoons olive oil

Also needed:

8 sticks from nontoxic wood (such as hazelnut, willow, beech)

Charcoal briquettes, or embers from a campfire

I. In a bowl, mix the flour, dry yeast, salt, garlic salt, Italian herbs, and sugar.

II. Add the water and oil and knead into a smooth dough that loosens from the inside of the bowl by itself. Cover with a clean dish towel and let rise in a warm spot until the dough has doubled in size, approximately 1 hour.

III. Separate the dough into 8 pieces of equal size, arrange them onto a baking sheet lined with parchment paper and let rest for another 15 minutes.

IV. In the meantime, prepare fuel for fire.

V. Roll each dough ball into a long rope and, beginning at the top end, seamlessly wrap each one closely around one of the sticks. Tightly pinch the dough at both ends to prevent it from coming off during baking.

VI. Hold sticks about 8 inches from fuel. Slowly turn sticks until bread is golden brown and done all the way through, about 5 to 8 minutes

Tip

Stick breads may also be baked in a 400° oven. Arrange them on a baking sheet lined with parchment paper and bake until golden brown, approximately 15 minutes, turning once.

Tater Salad

Level	Prep Time	Cook Time
Easy	2 hours	45 minutes

Serves 4

20 ounces potatoes (waxy)

½ stick butter

4 ounces bacon strips

2 onions, finely diced

¼ cup white wine vinegar

⅔ cup veal stock

1 tablespoon Dijon mustard

¼ cup sunflower seed oil

Salt

White pepper, freshly ground

3 stems Italian parsley, finely chopped

I. Cook the potatoes a day ahead. Place them in a large pot and cover with water. Put the lid on the pot, and bring to a boil. Reduce heat to low, and let simmer for 15 minutes. Drain and let cool overnight.

II. Peel the potatoes and cut them into slices about ⅛ inch thick. Add them to a large bowl.

III. Melt the butter in a pan on medium heat. Add the bacon strips and fry them until golden brown on both sides, 3 to 4 minutes. Add the onions and cook for 3 minutes. Deglaze with white wine vinegar and veal stock. Stir in the mustard. Reduce heat to low and let simmer for 3 minutes. Pour in the oil while constantly stirring the mixture.

IV. Pour the hot marinade on top of the potato slices and combine well. Season to taste with salt and pepper, cover the bowl with plastic wrap, and let marinate in refrigerator for at least 2 hours.

V. Immediately before serving the tater salad, add chopped parsley and mix one more time.

Mirkwood Batwings

Level	Prep Time	Cook Time
Easy	20 minutes, plus 3 hours for marinading	50 minutes

Serves 4

1 tablespoon dried sage

1 tablespoon dried rosemary

2 tablespoons dried thyme

2 tablespoons ground paprika

1 tablespoon salt

1 tablespoon cayenne pepper

¾ cup teriyaki sauce with roasted garlic

½ cup soy sauce

¼ cup buttermilk

3 drops black food gel

2 pounds chicken wings

Also needed:

Large resealable freezer bag

I. Add the sage, rosemary, thyme, paprika, salt, cayenne pepper, teriyaki sauce, soy sauce, buttermilk, and the food gel to a small bowl and blend well. Transfer the mixture into a sealable freezer bag.

II. Rinse the chicken wings with cold water, pat them dry with paper towels, and add them to the freezer bag. Seal bag, massage the marinade into the meat, and let sit in refrigerator for at least 3 hours and preferably overnight.

III. Remove the chicken wings from the marinade. Add the marinade to a small pot and reduce it on medium heat for 30 minutes, stirring constantly, until it turns into a glossy dark sauce. Remove from heat and let cool slightly.

IV. In the meantime, preheat oven to 325°. Slide a wire rack onto middle rail and place a large bowl partially filled with water beneath it to catch drippings.

V. Generously brush the chicken wings with reduced marinade and place them directly on wire rack. Loosely cover them with foil and roast for 40 to 45 minutes, turning them every 10 minutes and brushing them with more sauce. Remove foil, brush chicken wings with the remaining sauce, and heat broiler to 425° to nicely crisp the skin, about 5 minutes. Remove the "batwings" from oven and serve them immediately.

Dwarf-style Beetroot

Level	Prep Time	Cook Time
Easy	10 minutes	40 minutes

Serves 4

For the chickpeas:

6 ounces chickpeas (canned), drained

2 tablespoons canola oil

1 teaspoon salt

1 teaspoon ground sweet paprika

1 teaspoon turmeric

1 teaspoon ground caraway seeds

1 teaspoon ground cumin

For the beetroot soup:

2 tablespoons coconut oil

¾ cup onions, finely diced

1 garlic clove, finely minced

1 tablespoon ginger, freshly grated

1 pound beetroot, precooked and julienned

2 tablespoons medium-hot curry powder

1¼ cups vegetable stock

2 cups beetroot juice

1 tablespoon tandoori paste

½ cup coconut milk (unsweetened)

2 tablespoons lime juice

Salt

Pepper

Fresh cilantro, for garnish

Preparing the chickpeas:

I. Dab the chickpeas dry with a paper towel. In a bowl, combine them with the canola oil, salt, paprika, turmeric, caraway seeds, and cumin.

II. Heat a nonstick pan on medium heat. Add the chickpeas, roast them for 15 to 20 minutes, tipping the pan but not stirring so they remain whole. As soon as they are nicely browned and crispy, put them on a paper towel to drain. Let cool for a moment.

Preparing the beetroot soup:

III. Heat the coconut oil in a large pot on medium heat. Add the onions, garlic, and ginger and cook until translucent. Add the beetroot and stir, cooking for another 2 minutes. Add curry powder and cook briefly, then pour in the vegetable stock and beetroot juice, and let simmer for 10 minutes, stirring occasionally.

IV. Add the tandoori paste, coconut milk, and lime juice to the pot and let simmer for another 5 to 6 minutes. Season to taste with salt and pepper.

V. Ladle soup in 4 bowls and garnish with cilantro leaves and roasted chickpeas.

Hobbit Head Cheese

Level	Prep Time	Cook Time
Easy	10 minutes	120 minutes, plus 2 hours for resting

Serves 6 to 8

4 cups plus 5 tablespoons water

Salt

1 pound pork meat (such as shoulder or belly)

1 onion, finely diced

10 ounces frozen soup greens

1 large pickle, roughly chopped

1 bay leaf

3 peppercorns

½ cup vinegar

Sugar

1 package dry gelatin

Parsley, very finely diced

Also needed:

Loaf pan (about 4 by 10 inches)

I. In a large pot, bring 4 cups of heavily salted water to a boil. Add the pork, onion, soup greens, pickle, bay leaf, and peppercorns. Simmer uncovered for about 1½ hours, until the meat is done, occasionally skimming off the foam that rises to the surface during cooking.

II. Remove the meat from the stock and let it cool. Using a large, sharp knife, cut the meat into small cubes. Pour the stock through a colander into a clean container and ladle 1½ cups of it into a pot. Add the vinegar and season to taste with salt and sugar.

III. In a small bowl, mix the dry gelatin with 5 tablespoons of cold water and let soak for 10 minutes.

IV. Bring the vinegar broth to a boil, remove it from heat, and add the gelatin. Stir until the gelatin has dissolved, then add the cubed pork and about 1 cup of the cooked greens.

V. Rinse loaf pan with cold water. Fill it with the head cheese mixture. Smooth the surface and evenly sprinkle it with finely chopped parsley. Cover with plastic wrap, let congeal, and let set in refrigerator for about 2 hours.

VI. When the head cheese is firm, loosen it with a knife along the edges of the pan and carefully turn it over onto a plate.

DRINKS

Beorn's Honey Milk..................................136

Ent Potion..138

Miruvor 140

Athelas Tea...142

The Old Took's Hot Chocolate 144

Miruvóre..146

Orc Brew...148

Old Winyard's Mulled Wine 150

Beorn's Honey Milk

Level	Prep Time
Easy	2 minutes

Makes 1 cup

1 tablespoon honey

1 pinch ground cinnamon

1 tablespoon pistachios, finely chopped, and more, roughly chopped, for garnish

1½ cups whole milk

Ice cubes

I. In a small bowl, whisk the honey, cinnamon, finely chopped pistachios, and milk until foamy.

II. Add a couple of ice cubes to a cup. Fill it up with the honey milk and garnish with roughly chopped pistachios.

III. Serve immediately.

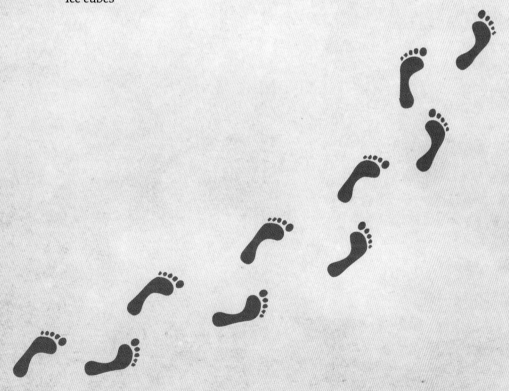

Ent Potion

Level	Prep Time
Easy	10 minutes

Serves 4 (about 1 quart)

1 organic lime

2 large kiwis, peeled and diced

1 cucumber, peeled and diced

2 green apples, diced

2 ounces lamb's lettuce

2 tablespoons honey

2 stems fresh mint

1 cup cold water

I. Wash the lime with hot water, dry it off, and zest and juice it.

II. In a high-performance kitchen blender, finely puree the kiwi, cucumber, lime zest, apples, lamb's lettuce, honey, and mint with 3 tablespoons of lime juice and 8 ounces of cold water.

III. Store the potion in refrigerator. Enjoy it slightly cooled.

Miruvor

Level	Prep Time	Cook Time
Difficult	9–10 weeks	120 minutes, including time for resting

Makes about 3 quarts

3 cups apple juice
(unfiltered)

½ teaspoon yeast

2½ quarts water

3 pounds honey

2½ tablets yeast-feeding
salt (about 0.3 ounces)

1 ounce St. John's wort

½ ounce meadowsweet

⅓ ounce verbena

¼ teaspoon silica sol
(available at pharmacies)

Also needed:

Demijohn (about 1½ gallons
including fermentation
attachment and rubber
stopper)

Kitchen thermometer

Bottles

I. Sterilize demijohn and all other utensils, either by boiling them in hot water (if a large enough pot is available) or thoroughly rinsing them with a food-safe disinfectant such as a soda solution. (If using the latter method, rinse with clean water afterward.)

II. To prepare the yeast culture, pour 8 ounces of the apple juice into a sterile container, carefully stir in the yeast, cover, and let sit in a warm place for about 90 minutes.

III. In the meantime, boil the water in a large pot, then let it cool below 80°. (The yeast will not survive higher temperatures.) Add the water, honey, remaining apple juice, and yeast-feeding salt to a large container, and stir well. Fold in the yeast culture. Using a funnel, pour the mixture into the sterile demijohn. Add the St. John's wort, meadowsweet, and verbena. Seal the demijohn with its rubber stopper, and let sit in a warm spot for 4 weeks. During this time, swirl the liquid in the demijohn at least once every day to prevent the yeast from settling, but do not open it.

IV. Ferment the mixture for another 4 weeks, but don't move the demijohn anymore. The fermenting process is over when no more small bubbles rise inside of the fermentation tube. Open the demijohn and add the silica sol, which will purge the yeast and sink to the bottom. Let sit for another week, then pour the liquid through a fine sieve into sterilized bottles. Tightly sealed, it will keep for about 3 months.

Athelas Tea

Level	Prep Time	Cook Time
Easy	70 minutes, including time for drying	10 minutes

Makes several pots

Peel of 2 organic clementines (dried)

1 vanilla bean

1 stick cinnamon, roughly chopped

5 star anise, roughly chopped

5 cloves, roughly chopped

1 tablespoon grated licorice

4 ounces black tea

2 tablespoons raspberry syrup

I. For this blend of tea, you'll need dried clementine peel, which is not available at stores. Wash the clementines with hot water, dry them off, peel them, and cut the peelings into small cubes. Spread the cubes onto a baking sheet lined with parchment paper and let them dry in a warm, dry place for a couple of days or in an oven preheated to 325° for 1 hour.

II. Combine the vanilla bean, cinnamon, star anise, cloves, licorice, clementine peels, and black tea in a small bowl. Pour the blend into a tea tin, where it'll keep for a few months.

III. To prepare the tea, put 4 to 5 teaspoons of the blend in a tea ball, hang in a teapot, pour in boiling water, and let it steep for 4 to 5 minutes, depending on desired strength. Take out the tea ball and stir in the raspberry syrup.

IV. Serve immediately.

The Old Took's Hot Chocolate

Level	Prep Time	Cook Time
Easy	5 minutes	10 minutes

Serves 2

¼ cup heavy cream

2 cups milk

2 tablespoons unsweetened cocoa

2 teaspoons vanilla sugar

3 ounces dark chocolate, roughly chopped

Chocolate shavings

I. In a mixing bowl, whisk the cream until stiff.

II. Put the milk, cocoa, vanilla sugar, and dark chocolate in a pot on medium heat and stir constantly until the chocolate has melted, taking care not to let the milk boil. Reduce heat if necessary.

III. Remove pot from heat and let cool for 2 to 3 minutes. Stir well one more time and pour the mixture into two cups or heat-resistant glasses. Add the whipped cream on top and sprinkle with the chocolate shavings.

IV. Serve immediately.

Miruvóre

Level	Prep Time	Cook Time
Easy	5 minutes	15 minutes

Makes about 4 cups

6 to 7 fresh peaches,
pitted and cubed

¾ cup sugar

1¼ cups water

Zest of 1 organic lemon

2 cups carbonated lemon soda

Crushed ice (optional)

I. Add the peaches, sugar, and water to a pot on medium heat and bring to a boil, stirring constantly. Add the lemon zest. Let simmer until the sugar has dissolved and the fruit pulp is very soft, about 8 to 10 minutes. Remove from heat and let cool slightly.

II. Pour the peach syrup through a sieve into a bowl, then pour it into a large pitcher and fill pitcher with lemon soda. Cover and cool in refrigerator. It is best served with some crushed ice.

III. The lemonade keeps up to 3 days in refrigerator.

Orc Brew

Attention!
Uses Alcohol

Level	Prep Time
Easy	2 minutes

Makes 1 brew

5 to 6 fresh raspberries

5 to 6 fresh blackberries

Crushed ice

1½ tablespoons vanilla liqueur

1½ tablespoons gin

1½ tablespoons lime juice

¼ cup passion fruit juice

¼ cup cherry juice

¼ cup banana juice, ice-cold

I. In a small bowl, roughly crush the raspberries and blackberries with a spoon.

II. Pour crushed ice into a large pitcher.

III. Add the vanilla liqueur, gin, and lime juice and mix.

IV. Add the crushed berries. Stir in the passion fruit juice, cherry juice, and banana juice.

V. Serve immediately.

Old Winyard's Mulled Wine

Level	Prep Time	Cook Time
Easy	2 minutes	20 minutes

Makes 3 to 4 cups

4 cups dry red wine

¼ cup cane sugar

8 cloves

2 cinnamon sticks, halved

6 star anise

3 cardamom pods

½ cup Amaretto

1 blood orange, sliced

2 tablespoons
dried cranberries

1 dash lemon juice

I. Heat the red wine and sugar in a pot on medium heat until the sugar has dissolved.

II. Add the cloves, cinnamon sticks, star anise, and cardamom pods to the pot, and let simmer for 10 minutes. Add the Amaretto. Reserve 4 orange slices for garnish, and add the remaining ones to the pot. Add the cranberries and lemon juice, and let simmer for another 5 minutes.

III. Remove the cloves, cinnamon sticks, cardamom pods, and star anise from the pot. Keep the cinnamon sticks for garnish.

IV. Pour the mulled wine into 3 or 4 cups. Add a half cinnamon stick to each one. Garnish the cups with orange slices and serve immediately.

Acknowledgments

So, the work is done. All the dishes have been cooked, all the photos have been taken, and all the recipes have been written. Now, it is time for a confession: It took me three or four attempts to finally read J. R. R. Tolkien's masterpiece, *The Lord of the Rings*. Although Tolkien's trilogy is (rightly so!) considered a classic of fantasy literature and has significantly influenced many writers I always admired, I had a fair number of issues with it—or, more precisely, with its, let's say, rather tedious prologue, "Concerning Hobbits," which put me off time and again. I was young and naive and told myself, "If the entire book is like this, then count me out! I can't take that for a thousand small-printed pages!"

And that is how it came about that I put the novel aside numerous times, unnerved by it and asking myself why the rest of the world thought so highly of that book. Not until I fought my way through the prologue years later and finally got to the actual story did the unparalleled charm of Middle-earth reveal itself to me. Ever since, I've read the book just as regularly as I have watched *Back to the Future* (in my eyes, the best movie of all time, right after Peter Jackson's congenial screen adaptation of *The Lord of the Rings*), and my fascination with it still keeps growing. It seems, the true depth and meaning of Tolkien's ring saga would not reveal themselves to me until I had reached a certain age. Some things, it seems that one realizes not until later, in looking back and recalling the past.

Along these lines, I would like to use the opportunity to thank all those people without whom you would not hold this book in your hands. First, credit is due to the team at DK. Monika Schlitzer led the way by bringing this project across the finish line with enthusiasm, foresight, and a steady hand. Credit also goes to Doreen Wolff, Heike Fassbender, Bruni Thiemeyer, Carmen Brand, Nicole Walter, and all the other good souls at the publishers, who were on hand with help and advice at all times.

In addition, my sincere thanks go to the following people: Dimitrie Harder, the best photographer in the world, who captures on camera all the crazy ideas that roam through my head. Jo Löffler and Holger "Holle" Wiest, my two "Dinos," without whom nothing would be as it is (and the same is true of Roberts "Rob" Urlovskis). Ulrich Peste, for many wonderful moments all over the world. Raoul Goff, Steve Jones, Vanessa Lopez, Chrissy Kwasnik, and the editorial team at Insight Editions. Thomas and Alexandra Stamm, who, more and more, turn into friends (and that says a lot in my case). My brother from another mother, Thomas Böhm, and Gabi, Susi, and Tommy; Tobias, Andrea, Lea, Finja, and that guy she now lives with, Jannik or Jannis or something like that. Katharina "the one true cat" Böhm, for more reasons than I could name, and Annelies Haubold. In memoriam, the unequaled Oskar "Ossi" Böhm, the father I never had. And especially my family, who keep giving me opportunities to go on adventures like this one and make my existence meaningful.

Everything you like about this book, please thank these wonderful people. For any slips or inaccuracies or too much celery salt, you are welcome to blame me and nobody else but me.

Tom Grimm

About the Author and Photographer

TOM GRIMM

Tom Grimm, born in 1972, finished an apprenticeship in bookselling and works as an author, translator, journalist, editor, and producer for a large number of international book and newspaper publishers. He is fascinated with literature, movies, and video games. He loves amusement parks, traveling, and grilling experiments throughout the entire year. Just recently, he received the World Cookbook Award for his work. He lives and works in a small town in the Wiehen Hills near Bielefeld, Germany—which, despite all rumors to the contrary, does exist—with his family, a pack of wild cats, and life-size statues of Batman, Kung Fu Panda, Rayman, and the Orc Thrall.

DIMITRIE HARDER

Dimitrie Harder was born in 1977, the second child of a Russian mother and a German father, in Kyrgyzstan in Central Asia, which is characterized not only by its magnificent mountain panoramas but also by its culture, rich in myths and sagas. In 1990, his family moved to Germany, where he later discovered his passion for photography, a hobby that he eventually turned into a profession. Being enormously patient and full of love for details, he is able to put himself into almost any kind of mood that the worlds he is moving in with his photography ask for. He loves to bike, run, and hike; he despises wasting food; and he is the only person in the world who has ever called his partner in crime, Tom Grimm, officially a lout.

Recipe Index

BAKED GOODS

Bannock Bread 56

Beorn's Honey Cakes 14

Beren's Bread Flower 16

Bilbo's Crunchy Cookies 84

Bilbo's Eleventy-First Birthday Cake 92

Bilbo's Famous Seed Cake 74

Cram 26

Crickhollow Apple Cakelets 48

Elvish Bread 42

Fish in Bread Dough 76

Fruitcake 28

Hobbiton Pumpkin Rolls 24

Lembas 38

Orcish Stick Bread 124

Pumpkin Pastries 54

Sweet Mini Bundt Cakes 86

The One Ring 98

MEATS

Gimli's Salted Pork 112

Haradrim Tagine 102

Hobbit Head Cheese 132

Hobbit Shanks 110

Juniper Roast Lamb 118

Mirkwood Batwings 128

Orcish Hobbit Roast with Maggot Holes 120

Pippin's Lunch Snack 68

Pork Meat Pies 80

Ranger-style Quail 64

Rosemary Lamb Skewers 114

Sam's Coney Stew 108

Sam's Second Breakfast 34

Smoked Beans Skillet 62

Túrin Turambar's Tarragon Chicken 51

FISH

Brandywine Fish Casserole 66

Fish in Bread Dough 76

Garlicky Mussels from the Grey Havens 70

Herbed Trout on a Stick................................ 106

Númenórean Gilthead Seabram 116

DRINKS

Athelas Tea...142

Beorn's Honey Milk..................................... 136

Ent Potion...138

Miruvor 140

Miruvóre 146

Old Winyard's Mulled Wine 150

Orc Brew 148

The Old Took's Hot Chocolate 144

SAVORIES

Beorn's Baked Cheese...............................44

Brandywine Fish Casserole 66

Breakfast Patties....................................... 18

Dwarf-style Beetroot.............................. 130

Farmer Maggot's Mushroom Ragout 40

Fish in Bread Dough 76

Fluffy Mashed Potatoes...........................78

Garlicky Mussels from the Grey Havens 70

Gimli's Salted Pork.................................. 112

Haradrim Tagine 102

Herbed Trout on a Stick................................ 106

Hobbit Head Cheese.................................132

Hobbit Shanks..110

Hobbiton Pumpkin Rolls.........................24

Juniper Roast Lamb 118

Mirkwood Batwings 128

Númenórean Gilthead Seabram 116

Orcish Hobbit Roast with Maggot Holes 120

Oven Spuds in Chive Sauce 60
Pippin's Lunch Snack 68
Pork Meat Pies... 80
Pumpkin Pastries 54
Ranger-style Quail 64
Root Vegetable Stew 104
Rosemary Lamb Skewers...114
Sam's Coney Stew 108
Sam's Second Breakfast..34
Smoked Beans Skillet 62
Spud Cakes 32
Sweet Chestnut Soup..96
Tater Salad 126
The Prancing Pony's Tater Soup.................................. 72
Túrin Turambar's Tarragon Chicken 51

SWEETS

Beorn's Honey Cakes.. 14
Bilbo's Crunchy Cookies...84
Bilbo's Eleventy-First Birthday Cake............................92
Bilbo's Famous Seed Cake 74
Cram...26
Crickhollow Apple Cakelets 48
Filled Oven Pears 88
Gandalf's Nut Pudding.. 90
Home-Canned Peaches...46
Millet Gruel 12
Pancakes 20
Rivendell Fig Treats 30
Sweet Mini Bundt Cakes..86

VEGETARIAN

Beorn's Baked Cheese...44
Beorn's Honey Cakes.. 14
Breakfast Patties 18
Cram...26

Crickhollow Apple Cakelets 48

Dwarf-style Beetroot 130

Elvish Bread 42

Fluffy Mashed Potatoes 78

Fruitcake 28

Hobbiton Pumpkin Rolls 24

Home-Canned Peaches 46

Lembas 38

Millet Gruel 12

Oven Spuds in Chive Sauce 60

Pancakes 20

Pumpkin Pastries 54

Rivendell Fig Treats 30

Root Vegetable Stew 104

Sweet Chestnut Soup..96

Po box 15
Cobb, CA 95426
©2022 Reel Ink Press

Isbn: 978-1-958862-00-1

Originally published as *Das Inoffizielle Mittelerde Kochbuch*
© 2022 DK Verlang Dorling Kindersley.
Created by Grinning Cat Productions.

Manufactured in china

10 9 8 7 6 5 4 3 2 1